Peace of Heart in All Things

G-6513

Peace of Heart in All Things

Meditations for Each Day of the Year

Brother Roger of Taizé

GIA

GIA Publications, Inc.
Chicago

GIA

G-6513
Distributed in North America
exclusively by
GIA Publications, Inc.
7404 S. Mason Ave.
Chicago, IL 60638
www.giamusic.com

ISBN: 1-57999-384-2

Printed in U.S.A.

Table of Contents

About this Book

In this book, the founder of Taizé offers a brief meditation for each day of the year. These short texts attempt to express realities that we can return to, day after day, our whole life long.

This book also contains a hundred or so prayers, printed in *italics*. They are often expressed in the first person plural. When they are used for personal meditation, the "we" naturally becomes "I."

The texts for Holy Week and Pentecost have been placed between the months of March and April since the dates change every year.

At the end of the book can be found a number of Bible passages dealing with trust and peace of heart.

Preface

This book was written for those who aspire to maintain peace of heart in all things, living in joy, simplicity, and mercy.

With very little, sometimes with just a few words reduced to the essential, it is possible to go forward day after day.

When disenchantment gains the upper hand and our steps grow heavy, when a fine human hope vanishes, then peace of heart is more indispensable than ever.

I have written these pages as much for myself as for those who will read them.

God of mercy, we are yearning for peace of heart. And the Gospel allows us to glimpse that, even in hours of darkness, you love us and you want happiness for us.

January

January 1

Whoever is on a journey towards God goes from one beginning to another beginning. Will you be among those who dare to tell themselves: "Begin again! Leave discouragement behind! Let your soul live!"?

January 2

Christ never sets us up as judges of one another. The Gospel makes us concerned to love and to say it with our life.

January 3

Jesus, light of our hearts, ever since you rose from the dead, by the Holy Spirit you have never stopped coming to us. Whatever point we may be at, you are always waiting for us. And you tell us: "Come to me, you who are overburdened, and you will find relief."[1]

January 4

For those who discover Saint John, the most captivating thing is to glimpse this radiant insight: "God is love."[2] And Christ did not come to earth to judge the world but so that, through him, the Risen Lord, every human being might be saved and reconciled.[3]

January 5

Alleviating human suffering is at the heart of the Gospel. When we allay other people's trials, we do it for Christ himself; he is the one we encounter. "Whatever you do for the least of my brothers and sisters," he says, "you do for me."[4]

January 6

Even if you seem to have very little faith, will you prepare yourself to welcome a Gospel light? "It shines in the darkness and the darkness was unable to put it out."[5]

January 7

God of every human being, you never impose yourself, you never force our heart, but you place your peaceful light within each one of us.

January 8

There are countries where visible "homes for the dying" are to be found. In Western civilization, in addition, there are "homes for the dying" that are invisible. Children and young people there are marked for life because they have been abandoned; they are affected down to their very depths by broken relationships, by lack of affection. Their hearts are sometimes dying of loneliness. They feel as if they are on an ocean with no lighthouse. Some even reach the point of losing all desire to live. Are not situations of human abandonment one of the deepest traumas of our time?

January 9

In all things, peace of heart, serene joy. Centuries before Christ, a believer had already prayed with these words: "In God alone my soul finds rest, my hope comes from him; God alone is an unshakeable support."[6] And in the Gospel, Christ gives us this assurance: "Peace is my gift to you; I leave you my peace. Do not let your hearts be troubled or afraid."[7]

January 10

Six centuries before Christ, a Christian thinker, Isaac of Nineveh, wrote these words of fire: "All God can do is give his love." Those who understand this luminous reality begin to ask themselves: How can I communicate such a solid hope?

January 11

Breath of Christ's loving, Holy Spirit, in the depths of our soul you set faith. It is like a surge of trusting repeated countless times in the course of our life. It can only be a simple act of trust, so simple that it is accessible to all.

January 12

To let ourselves be refreshed by living water welling up inside us, it is good to go off for a few days in silence and peace.

Long ago Elijah, the believer, set out in search of a place where he could listen to God. He climbed a mountain in the wilderness. A hurricane arose, the earth began to shake, a conflagration broke out. Elijah knew that God was not in these outbursts of nature. God is never the author of earthquakes or natural disasters. Then everything became quiet, and there was the murmur of a gentle breeze. Elijah covered his face. He had come to the realization that God's voice also made itself understood in a breath of silence.[8]

January 13

Some brothers of our community have been living in Bangladesh for many years, sharing the lives of the poorest people. One of them wrote, "After a cyclone, our neighbors asked us: 'Why all these misfortunes? Have we sinned against God so much?'" What made their suffering worse was the secret fear of a punishment from God.

God never causes fear, anguish, or distress. He shares the suffering of those going through incomprehensible trials. And he enables us in our turn to alleviate the suffering of others. God wants neither wars, nor natural catastrophes, nor the violence of accidents. God is innocent of all this; God is innocence.

January 14

A luminous Gospel insight has come to light after gathering dust for a long time: "The Risen Christ is united to every human being without exception, even if they are not aware of it."[9]

January 15

God of all loving, you fill us with the freshness of the Gospel when a heart that trusts is at the beginning of everything.

January 16

Happy those who can make this prayer their own: Christ, you see who I am. For me, not to hide anything in my heart from you is a necessity. You were a human being, too. And when my inner self seems to be pulled in a thousand different directions, my thirsting heart reaches the point of praying: "Enable me to live a life rooted in you, Jesus the Christ; unify my desire and my thirst."

January 17

Where would we be today if certain women, men, young people, and also children had not arisen at moments when the human family seemed destined for the worst? They did not say: "Let things take their course!" Beyond the confrontations between persons, peoples, and spiritual families, they prepared a way of trusting. Their lives bear witness to the fact that human beings have not been created for hopelessness.

January 18

Love is a word that is often abused. Love is easy to say. To practice a love that forgives is another thing altogether.

January 19

Jesus, our joy, by remaining in your presence, we realize that the Gospel calls us to give our life. Even if we forget you, your love remains, and you send your Holy Spirit upon us.

January 20

From the time of the apostles, the Virgin Mary, and the first believers, there has been a call to live in great simplicity and to share. One of the pure joys of the Gospel is to go further and further toward a simplicity of heart that leads to a simplicity of living.

January 21

Simplifying never means choosing an ice-cold austerity, without kindheartedness, filled with judgments upon those who do not take the same road. If simplicity of life became equated with gloom, how could it lead us to the Gospel? The spirit of simplicity shines through in signs of serene joy, and also in cheerfulness of heart. Simplifying invites us to arrange what little we have in creation's simple beauty.

January 22

With almost nothing, above all through the gift of our lives, the Risen Christ desires that both fire and Spirit be made perceptible in us.[10] However poor we may be, let us not quench the fire, let us not quench the Spirit.[11] In them, the wonder of a love bursts into flame. And the humble trusting of faith is communicated like fire spreading from one person to the next.

January 23

Jesus, our trust, your Gospel brings with it such a fine hope that we would like to give ourselves to the very end in order to follow you. And irresistibly the question arises: Where is the source of such hope? It lies in surrendering ourselves to you, Christ.

January 24

One day in Taizé, a child said, "My father left us. I never see him, but I still love him and at night I pray for him." Without realizing it, that child was living the miracle of kindheartedness.

January 25

Whoever seeks reconciliation with a simple heart is able to pass through rock-hard situations like the water of a stream that, in early springtime, makes its way through the still-frozen ground.

January 26

An Orthodox theologian from Bucharest, Father Staniloae, who had been in prison for his beliefs, wrote words so essential that we would like to know them by heart: “I looked for God in the human beings of my village, then in books and in ideas. But that brought me neither peace nor love. One day, while reading the Church Fathers, I discovered that it was actually possible to encounter God through prayer. I gradually realized that God was close to me, that he loved me, and that, filled by his love, my heart opened to others. I realized that love was a communion, with God and with others. And that, without this communion, everything is only sadness and desolation.”

January 27

Holy Spirit, mystery of a presence, you bathe us in unfailing kindness. It allows a life of humble trusting to blossom in us…and our hearts become lighter.

January 28

Self-mastery out of love for others keeps us alert. This may be the price we pay for peace of heart, both for others and for ourselves: not letting ourselves be overcome by emotions or impressions that are so often magnified by the imagination.

January 29

When darkness and doubts assail you, why not keep them at arm's length? Often they are only interludes of unbelief, nothing more. Why see yourself as dry ground? When his dew appears, the tears of the morning, a thirst is quenched in the desert of your soul.

January 30

Could there be a chasm of fears and of doubts inside us? Joy! Joy of the soul! The depths of worry in us call out to other depths,[12] the inexhaustible compassion of his love. And what a surprise: trust was at hand, and so often we were unaware of it.

January 31

Christ Jesus, when we think we are alone, you are present. If there seems to be doubt within us, that does not make you love us any the less. We would like to be daring enough to take risks on account of you, Christ. So we pay attention to your words: "Those who give their life for love of me will find it."[13]

February

February 1

Nothing is more beautiful than a face made transparent by a whole lifetime of sorrows and joys, of combats, and of inner peace.

February 2

When Mary and Joseph presented Jesus in the Temple, they only had two doves to offer.[1] Are we not the poor of the Gospel, too, feeling our way forward as we search for God? And are not God's eyes especially attentive to what is fragile in us?

February 3

God of peace, you do not want us to know relentless worry but rather a humble repentance of heart. It is like a surge of trusting that enables us to place our burdens in you. And then, by the light of forgiveness, we discover a peace of heart.

February 4

So many Christians find in prayer the courage to take on responsibilities. Rooting themselves in the very wellsprings of Christ, they run the risks of faith.

February 5

One day Saint Teresa of Avila and Saint John of the Cross came together for a meal. Grapes were brought in. "I am not going to eat any," stated John of the Cross. "Too many people have none." "I, on the contrary, will eat some," replied Teresa of Avila, "in order to praise God for these grapes."

February 6

Christ of compassion, through your Gospel we discover that measuring what we are or what we are not leads nowhere. What matters is the humble trusting of faith. By it we are led to understand that "all God can do is give his love."

February 7

Happy the person who, at grips with an uncomfortable situation, dares to say, "I am like a bird singing in a thorn bush."[2] Doesn't the Gospel invite us to welcome the Holy Spirit in that part of ourselves where our childhood heart is still to be found?

February 8

As you walk in Christ's footsteps, do not be surprised at his words: "Whoever puts his hand to the plough cannot look back."[3] He invites you to leave behind bitterness, regrets, all that corrodes eternity's yes. Could this yes become worn out? Will it no longer keep you awake your whole life long?

February 9

Could we think we have given up on Christ? He never gives up on us. Do we feel we have abandoned him? He is present. That is something we never expected. That is more than we could ever hope for.

February 10

Jesus, our trust, ever since your resurrection, your light has been shining within us. And so we can still tell you: "We love you without having seen you, though we still do not see you we believe, and you seek to shower upon us a joy beyond words which already transfigures us."[4]

February 11

When timidity keeps you from asking for forgiveness, why not dare to make a simple gesture that does not need words? Put out your hand so the other person can make the sign of forgiveness in it, the sign of the cross.

February 12

Prayer enables us to discover where to find rest for our soul. And we are shown a reality hidden from our eyes: by the mysterious presence of his Holy Spirit, Christ is always with us. And the heart, even when overwhelmed by trials, can begin to sing anew: "Your compassion has visited me."

February 13

O Christ, you are united to every human being without exception, even if they are unaware of it. Still more, risen from the dead, you come to heal the secret wound of the soul. And for each person, the gates of a heartfelt compassion are opened.

February 14

Peace begins within us. As early as in the fourth century, Saint Ambrose of Milan wrote, "Begin the work of peace within yourself so that, once you are at peace yourself, you can bring peace to others."[5]

February 15

Inconsistencies sometimes find their way into that communion of love that is the Body of Christ, his Church. They cause a lot of suffering. So then, are we going to run away? No, never. All we can do is to run towards it, to support a renewal in the People of God.

February 16

There is nothing naive about the spirit of childhood, about simplicity according to the Gospel. They are inseparable from discernment. They call for maturity. Far from being simplistic, they are steeped in clear-sightedness.

February 17

Jesus, our peace, by the Holy Spirit you always come to us. And in the deepest part of our soul, there is the wonder of a presence. Our prayer may be quite poor, but you pray even in the silence of our hearts.

February 18

Doubt can be corrosive. It can cast human beings down to the bottom of a well. But there is always a light still shining from above. The dark we experience is not the dead of night; it is not pitch-darkness. It does not inundate the whole of our being. The light of Christ still penetrates it.

February 19

When we open the Gospel, this thought can come to us: Jesus' words are like a very old letter written to me in an unknown language. Since the author of these words is Christ, someone who loves me, I try to understand their meaning, and I am going to put into practice in my life the little I can grasp.

February 20

Risen Jesus, in your Gospel we discover such a clear hope. It sustains faith even in situations where there seems to be no way out. This hope reinvents the world.

February 21

Children bring such happiness to our life! Who can express adequately what some of them can communicate, to the point of being a reflection of the invisible communion.

February 22

Some Eastern Christians are very attached to the prayer of the Name of Jesus. There are those for whom simply repeating the name Jesus expresses the fullness of a communion. Throughout the world, other Christians pray almost unceasingly with a few words: "Christ Jesus, do not let my darkness speak to me; let me welcome your love." Or else they repeat that age-old prayer: "Let nothing trouble you, God alone is enough." Or again, they pray at every moment: "A thirst fills my soul, to surrender everything to you, Christ." And they find peace in their longing.

February 23

People who try to follow Christ by a yes for an entire lifetime are not unaware that there are still weak points within them. In days when trust seems to vanish, they call to mind these Gospel words: "Follow me and you will find rest for your heart."[6]

February 24

Christ Jesus, Savior of every life, you do not want inner anguish for anyone. And you come to shed light on the mystery of human suffering by placing in us the comfort given by the Holy Spirit.

February 25

When the heart is wounded or humiliated, it finds peace by entrusting to God, without waiting a single moment, those who have offended or mistreated it.

February 26

In our lives, there are choices that come straight from the Gospel: forgiveness, reconciliation, or an inner struggle to remain faithful. Accomplished for the sake of Christ, these choices express to him our love.

February 27

Two centuries after Christ's death, a believer wrote, "The calling God gives to Christians is so beautiful that it is not possible for them to run away from it."[7] To run away from what? To run away from the responsibilities drawn from the wellsprings of the faith.

February 28

Jesus, our hope, even were we weak and destitute, our deepest desire would be to understand that you love us. You shed light on the road leading to heartfelt compassion. You tell us, as you told your disciples: "Turn to God and believe in the Gospel."

February 29

Without forgiveness, without reconciliation, is there any future for human beings? And without reconciliation, what future is there for Christians?

March

March 1

In our community life, we know that simplicity and kind-heartedness are indispensable values. They may be two of the most radiant facets of the beauty of a communion.

March 2

How vigilant we must be not to stick any labels on anyone's forehead! Having a rigid image of another person can paralyze the whole evolution of their personality.

March 3

Christ Jesus, from the beginning you were in God.[1] *Since the birth of humanity, you have been a living Word. When you came to live among us, you made the humble trusting of faith accessible. And the day is coming when we can say: "I belong to Christ, I am Christ's."*

March 4

Some Christians are utterly disconcerted when they hear that their faith is illusory. Then doubt can creep into the soul. But there is nothing alarming about doubt. Inner freedom will open a way from doubt towards trusting. The Gospel will always tell each one of us: "Seek, seek and you will find."

March 5

Could there be a period of dryness in our life? Tirelessly, God is seeking us. And we discover him as if for the first time. Even when he is rejected, he never refuses to remain alongside us. And like the almond tree that begins to blossom in the light of springtime, he makes even the deserts of our soul burst into flower.

March 6

With you, Christ, we go forward from the shadows towards the light. And the Holy Spirit comes so that peace may spring up in our hearts.

March 7

Prayer does not always cause an outpouring of love for Christ. When fervor evaporates, there are times when this reality becomes apparent: the Risen Christ is not the one who went away; I am the one who is absent.

March 8

Even young children can experience trust in Christ. Go into a place of worship with a child, stand before an icon with him or her, and the life of that child may be warmed by the glow of an invisible presence. A flame has been kindled. It may happen that, sooner or later, it will burn in their heart of hearts.

March 9

Wishing to possess happiness at all costs often causes it to vanish. Are not peace of heart and serene joy offered to those who go to the point of giving their lives for love of Christ?

March 10

God of all mercy, you bury our past in the heart of Christ and you are going to take care of our future.

March 11

The Gospel never calls us to gloom. It never views human beings with pessimism. Just the opposite. It attempts to awaken in us a peaceful joy.

March 12

There are people for whom God is so dazzling that they are blinded and consider themselves to be agnostics. What they know of God is above all his silence.

March 13

Peace of heart in all things. Our peace of heart communicates the gift of pacification to those around us. Peace of heart leads to serene joy. It is one of its sources.

March 14

Christ Jesus, you call us to give our life for love.[2] *And even if there is a greater or lesser degree of darkness in each of us, there is also your presence, your Holy Spirit.*

March 15

There is one thing we shall never fully understand: Fragile as we are, like vessels of clay, why did God call us to be bearers of Christ's hope? Because "the radiance comes from God, not from us."[3]

March 16

"All God can do is give his love." What God asks of us above all else is to surrender ourselves to him. And what a discovery! His compassion reawakens an inexhaustible goodness in our heart of hearts.

March 17

Holy Spirit, in communion with you, even when we seem to have received no answer to our prayer, through it you have already accomplished something within us.

March 18

All who journey from one beginning to another in a life of communion with Jesus, the Christ, do not focus on their own progress or backsliding. By day and by night, the Gospel seed, placed in the depths of their being, sprouts and grows.[4]

March 19

Does a Gospel joy withdraw from our life when we are affected by trials? When we are at the extreme point of heartfelt sorrow, a Gospel joy can be restored. It is comfort in the depths of our being.

March 20

Jesus, our peace, your Holy Spirit is a fire that never says "Enough!"[5] *You come to send that Spirit upon each of us, just as you did to your disciples after your resurrection.*

March 21

Even the valley of tears can become a place of living springs.[6] And then we are free, able to look at people and things with poetry...free to glimpse already on this earth the dawning of a life that will never end.

March 22

When changes in society come faster and faster, the older generations can be confronted with situations that are not easy to deal with. They need compassion, sometimes even consolation. How can we move forward without plunging the older generations into an abyss of worry at the same time?

March 23

When the silences of the soul make their appearance, resting in God is already a way of reaching that oasis where our thirsts are quenched.

March 24

Jesus, our hope, you turn us into the humble of the Gospel. Our deepest desire is to understand that what is best in each of us is built up through a simple trusting, and even a child can do it.[7]

March 25

When we are faced with the Gospel call to say yes for our entire lifetime, sometimes the question arises: "How can I remain faithful?" The yes fascinates, and at the same time, it can frighten. And we hesitate. But one day we are astonished to find ourselves on the road, walking in Christ's footsteps: the yes had already been placed in the very depths of our being by the Holy Spirit. Then we begin to understand Mary's response: "May it be done to me according to your word."[8]

March 26

Deserts of the heart do exist. But perhaps there are fewer of them than we think! Isn't the Holy Spirit, the Comforter, present in each one of us?

March 27

Looking back to what has wounded us, lingering over our failures, paralyzes us down to the fibers of the soul. In new beginnings, the Holy Spirit accomplishes a miracle—he sets us free, he blots out the past, he leads us to love.

March 28

Holy Spirit, comforting Spirit, happy are they who turn to you over and over again! And when we entrust to you, even without words, our lives and those of others, our longings find a Gospel response.

March 29

Chase away fleeting cares like a child blowing on a dry leaf. Don't cling to worries like a hand clutching the branch of a thorn bush; let go, and let Christ welcome you.[9]

March 30

Whatever point we may be at, the Risen Christ searches tirelessly for us. Do we hear him knocking at the door of our heart when he tells us: "Come, follow me."?[10]

March 31

Jesus, our peace, you try to be everything for us. And when temptation urges us to abandon you, Christ, poor and humble of heart, you pray within us.

Holy Week and Pentecost

Holy Thursday

The day before he was tortured on a cross, Jesus went off to pray in Gethsemane. He asks us, just as he asked his disciples, "Will you stay with me to keep watch and pray?"[1]

Good Friday

When our eyes are fixed on the face of Jesus hanging on the cross, we would like to tell him: "Savior of every human being, you knew failure in your life. Overwhelmed by sorrow, you did not threaten anyone.[2] And you bear our own trials with us."[3]

Holy Saturday

Christ Jesus, you go down to the lowest point of our human condition. Still more, you even go to visit those who died without having known anything about you when they were on earth.[4]

Easter Sunday

Christ Jesus, even if your resurrection kindles within us a flame that may be quite weak, it enables us to live in communion with you. And by your Gospel we realize that you came to earth not just for part of humankind, but for every human being, even if they are unaware of your presence within them.

Pentecost Sunday

Jesus, our peace, by your Holy Spirit you continue to be for us today what you were for your disciples on earth. In your Gospel, you assure us: "I will never leave you alone; I will send you the Holy Spirit as a support and a comfort, to remain with you forever."[5]

April

April 1

If Christ were not risen, he would not be present alongside us today. He would just be a remarkable personality in the history of humanity. It would not be possible to discover a communion in him, to share with him through prayer.

April 2

Joy and peace of heart are incomparable values for following Christ. Fear and worry can undermine the confident trusting of faith.

April 3

God, our Father, in humble prayer we remember the words one believer said to Jesus: "I believe, Lord, but come to help my lack of faith."[1] When a portion of unbelief remains within us, your mercy upholds our faith.

April 4

Whoever has experienced the approach of death in their youth senses that, even more than the body, it is the depths of the self that are first and foremost in need of healing. A childhood or youth fraught with trials can engender the boldness needed to run risks for the Gospel. Trust is at hand....

April 5

It sometimes happens that we go so far as to question Christ Jesus: "...But what is going on in me? Why these times when I grow weary in persevering? I am seeking you, so how can I linger over suggestions so foreign to the Gospel? Explain me to myself!"

April 6

When we pray, if we find that human language is almost incapable of expressing the depths of our being, then there is no need to be alarmed. In a prayer steeped in silence, we rest in God—body, soul, and spirit.

April 7

Jesus, joy of our hearts, you remain alongside us like someone who is poor and also as the Risen Lord. You want to turn us into people who are fully alive, not lukewarm. And every time a distance opens up between ourselves and you, you invite us to discover your presence, which is there for all without exception.

April 8

On the evening of his resurrection, Jesus came up to two of his disciples who were going to the village of Emmaus. But they did not realize that the Risen Christ was walking alongside them.[2] There are times in our life when we lose the awareness that, through the Holy Spirit, the Risen

Christ is with us. Whether recognized or not, he is present, even when nothing seems to suggest it.

April 9

If we could only realize in the simplicity of faith that Christ, risen from the dead, is above all else communion.... He did not come to start a new religion, but to offer every human being this mystery of a communion in his Body, his Church.

April 10

Jesus, Risen Lord, you welcome into endless life those who have gone before us. Already they are contemplating the invisible, and they sometimes remain so close to us. When there are times of sorrow, that makes you love us even more. And by your Holy Spirit, you comfort, you bring peace.

April 11

How many men and women think they never do enough for those entrusted to them! And so they judge themselves. Could they even go so far as to forget the words of Saint John: "If your heart condemns you, God is greater than your heart."?[3]

April 12

Who will open their eyes to the anguish of the innocent: children marked for life by broken relationships, by being abandoned, and also elderly people who are forced to live in unbearable loneliness? Who will run to join them?

April 13

God wants to make us living signs of his Christ. Through the Gospel, we realize that he calls us to communicate, by the lives we lead, a reflection of his love.

April 14

Christ, if you ask us, as in the Gospel, "Do you love me?," we stammer our reply: "You know that I love you, Christ,[4] *perhaps not as I would like to, but I do love you."*

April 15

Could not accompanying Christ in his Passover from death to life lead to discovering serene joy even at the heart of trials? When there is intense suffering, the heart can be broken, but it is not hardened.

April 16

When human beings grasp intuitively the beauty of creation, there can be a sense in which that takes hold of them, however partially. Is not contemplation an inner disposition in which the whole being is caught up in the wonder of a love, taken hold of by the infinite beauty of the living God?

April 17

God of all loving, why should we wait for our hearts to be changed in order to go to you? You transfigure them. In our wounds themselves you enable a communion with you to grow. And the gates of praise open within us.

April 18

A believer from Bangladesh, speaking about those around him who know nothing of Christ, said, "When the fire of God's love is in us, does it not shine all around us, even if we do not realize it?"

April 19

In his life on earth, Jesus needed to hear a human voice tell him, "You know that I love you." Three times he asked Peter, "Do you love me?"[5] Christ asks each of us the very same question, age-old and always new: "Do you love me?" And he asks each of us to be attentive to those he entrusts to us.

April 20

Inner silence and peace of heart never extinguish the call to human solidarity, which comes straight from the Gospel.

April 21

Holy Spirit, mystery of a presence, you breathe in us a gentle breeze that refreshes the soul. And the unexpected occurs: once again, we begin the journey from doubt towards the brightness of your light.

April 22

"Where there is love, God is present." If we can feel nothing, no need to waste time worrying about it. Where there is living mercy, God is present in fullness.

April 23

When we are assailed by feelings of inferiority, we may be surprised to come to this realization: The road to fulfillment lies not in prestigious gifts or great abilities, but in living love.

April 24

Jesus, our joy, when we pray in silence, without words, the simple desire for your presence is already the beginning of faith. And in our life, living water gushes forth: the goodness, the selflessness that come from the Holy Spirit.

April 25

When confronted with the calls of the Gospel, some people are beset by doubt and ask themselves, "Do I have enough faith?" But our faith did not create God. Nor will our doubts ever put an end to God's existence.

April 26

Christ does not turn us into people who have made it. He keeps us close to him, as transparent as the sky in springtime, a springtime just bursting into flower.

April 27

Even by night, we will go to the spring. In its depths there sparkles living water where we can quench our thirsts. Could the human soul be that, too: the secret heartbeat of a happiness almost beyond words?

April 28

Risen Jesus, sometimes our heart calls out to you like the believer in the Gospel: "I am not worthy to receive you, but only say the word and I will be healed."[6] *At the core of our life, your Gospel is light within us, your Eucharist is a presence within us.*

April 29

When we seem to lose the incentive to follow Christ, we can still surrender ourselves to the Holy Spirit, entrusting everything to him. May the day return when our heart and our spirit are like dry ground thirsting for him.... We kept on loving him, even when we had forgotten him.

April 30

Could glumness be more contagious than peace of heart? By looking at events pessimistically, some people attempt to acquire a certain authority. But doesn't this mean abandoning a Gospel treasure? Which one? Wonder, simplicity.

May

May 1

Happy are those who live in the trusting of faith: "They will see God!"[1] How will they see him? Not in a vision but like Mary who, attentive, "kept everything in her heart"[2] and saw God with her inward eye.

May 2

God of all eternity, you know that human language is almost incapable of expressing the longing for a communion with you. But you grant us the gift of your invisible presence. And the sun rises on a new day, a day of trusting.

May 3

In the fourth century, Ambrose, bishop of Milan, was deeply concerned to see that some Christians were accumulating riches. He wrote to them, "The earth was created in common and for everyone. Nature knows no wealthy people. You are not taking what is yours and giving it to the poor; you are restoring to them a portion of what belongs to them."[3]

May 4

Fragile and yet radiant, containing both the abyss and fullness, human beings are never doomed to despair. Hope can be glimpsed, even in a life overwhelmed by trials.

May 5

Jesus, light of the heart, we would never want to abandon you by our wayside. And when we let you transfigure our weaknesses, unexpected resources appear within us.

May 6

Would you only love those who love you? Almost anybody can do that, with no need for the Gospel. But Christ calls you to something that is almost incomprehensible: to love even those who hurt you and to pray for them.[4]

May 7

Attentive as we are to building up the human family, how can we remain unaware that there are people today who reflect the mysterious biblical figure of the "suffering servant"[5]: humiliated, ill-treated, with nothing to attract us, they bear our diseases.

May 8

When we pray, what can we do about distractions? Not worry about them. God is familiar with our longings. He perceives better than we do our intentions and what lies deep within our being.

May 9

Jesus, our peace, you enable us to walk by faith, to believe without having seen.[6] *And we persevere in our longing for an inner light that is there for everyone.*

May 10

When faced with age-old or brand-new divisions, is it not urgent today for Christians to be reconciled by love? And when Christ calls, who can refuse? How can we forget his words: "Be reconciled without delay."?[7] Do we have hearts large enough, imaginations open enough, love burning enough to enter upon that Gospel way: to live as people who are reconciled, without delaying a single day?

May 11

You aspire to follow the Risen Christ, and you wonder by what sign you will know that you have encountered him. Are you able to understand that he is always alive in the depths of your being, in your heart of hearts?

May 12

Christ Jesus, you did not come to earth to condemn the world but so that through you, the Risen Lord, every human being might find a path of communion.[8] *And when love goes to the point of forgiving, the heart, even when beset by trials, begins to live anew.*

May 13

The Gospel assures us that the Risen Christ is always with us.[9] We can ask him, "Show us the way." And he replies, "I am here." We tell him, "You understand my prayer; it is close to the prayer of a child." And the desire for a prayer that is utterly simple is always there within us.

May 14

Not resignation, but a trust that comes from the depths: surrendering ourselves to the Holy Spirit, entrusting again and yet again to him all that weighs upon our heart.

May 15

Submit to harsh events? No, consent to them instead. And supposing it even became possible to be built up inwardly through a trial....

May 16

Christ Jesus, you never lead us into discouragements that knock us off balance, but you enable us to achieve a communion with you. And though there may be trials in store for each person, there is, above all, compassion that comes from you. It brings us back to life.

May 17

Should we worry if we are not thinking about God all the time? Seven hundred years ago, a Christian from the Rhineland, called Meister Eckhart, wrote: "To turn to God…does not mean to keep thinking about God. That would be impossible…and in addition, it would not be the best thing. Human beings cannot be satisfied with a God that is the object of thought. For then, when the thought vanished, God would vanish, too…. God is beyond all human thoughts. And the reality of God never disappears."[10]

May 18

A reflection of Christ is in us. There is no point in trying to know what it consists in. So many people on earth radiate the holiness of Christ without realizing it and perhaps without even daring to believe it.

May 19

God of mercy, when we are bewildered by the incomprehensible suffering of the innocent, come to enable us to manifest, by the lives that we live, a reflection of the compassion of Christ.

May 20

A simple heart accepts that it cannot understand everything in the Gospel. It can say to God, "I am not relying on my own faith alone. Others understand what I cannot grasp, and they will shed light on my path."

May 21

There are elderly people full of selflessness who are absolutely essential for the younger generations. They listen, and in this way they unburden others of a load of worries. Spiritual mothers and fathers along the lines of the Gospel are given a hundredfold.

May 22

In the 1970s, social upheavals at times wounded something in the Christian consciousness. So many final judgments were passed, so much harshness expressed. This pressure even caused some people to stop believing in the worth of the life they had been living up to that point. In Taizé, we said: It is not for Christians to be "masters of worry." They are "servants of trust."

May 23

Searching for you, Christ, means discovering your presence even in the lonely places deep within us.[11] Happy those who surrender themselves to you.[12] Happy those who approach you with trusting hearts.

May 24

When tirelessly the Church listens, heals, and reconciles, it becomes what it is at its most luminous—a communion of love, of compassion, of consolation, a limpid reflection of the Risen Christ. Never distant, never on the defensive, freed from all forms of severity, the Church can let the humble trusting of faith shine right into our human hearts.

May 25

How many discoveries we shall make in the next world! We shall be astonished to meet people who, unacquainted with Christ, were living by him unawares.

May 26

Risen Christ, softly your words make themselves heard: "Why worry? Only one thing is necessary, a heart attentive to the Gospel and to the Holy Spirit."[13]

May 27

When the inner self is exhausted by regrets, it is embarked on self-destruction. Remaining in God in contemplative waiting opens the way to taking essential steps: consenting to our weak points, to our own limitations. Then what seemed insipid acquires a new taste. And peace of heart springs to life.

May 28

There is such a great need for us to be in communion with Christ. That communion reawakens an inner life in us. Living for Christ means choosing a life that is sometimes exposed, and not one that is turned in upon itself.

May 29

Jesus, hope of our hearts, when we realize that your love is shown above all in forgiveness, something in us is soothed and even transformed. We ask you: "What do you want from me?" And by the Holy Spirit, you reply: "Let nothing trouble you; dare to give your life."

May 30

Our prayer is a simple reality. Is it perhaps no more than a poor sigh? God hears us all the same. We should never forget that, at the heart of every person, the Holy Spirit is praying.[14]

May 31

Faith asks us neither to destroy nor to exalt human desire but to gather it into an even greater desire: the thirst for God. Yes, the simple desire for God is already the beginning of faith.

June

June 1

"I am living in you."[1] The Eucharist makes these words of Christ a reality even when the heart senses nothing, even for those who hardly dare hope it.

June 2

Savior of every life, in following you we choose to love and never to harden our hearts. And even were the depths of our being assailed by a trial, one way forward remains open—the way of serene trust.

June 3

In the middle of the twentieth century, there appeared a man named John, born in a humble peasant family in the north of Italy. When he announced the Second Vatican Council, that elderly man, John XXIII, pronounced words that are among the most crystal clear imaginable: "We will not try to find out who was wrong, we will not try to find out who was right, we will only say: Let us be reconciled!"[2]

During the last meeting we had with him shortly before his death, three of us from our community were present. We understood how deeply John XXIII wished us to be at peace concerning the future of our vocation. Making circular gestures with his hands, he explained, "The Catholic Church is made up of ever-larger concentric circles." Rather than giving in to worries, wasn't the essential already accomplished if we went forward in peace of heart?

June 4

During his life on earth, Jesus prayed and his face was transfigured by light. He also prayed with tears and pleading.

June 5

Christ Jesus, multitudes of children and young people have been marked for life because they were abandoned; they are like strangers on this earth. There are some who wonder: "Does my life still have any meaning?" And you assure us of this: each time you alleviate the suffering of an innocent person, you do it for me, Christ.[3]

June 6

There are physical forms of violence on earth, including war, torture, murder.... There are other more subtle forms of violence that are concealed in cunning tactics, in suspicion, mistrust, humiliation.... "There is no violence in God. God sent Christ not to accuse us, but to call us to himself, not to condemn us, but because he loves us."[4]

June 7

By forgiving us, God buries our past in the heart of Christ and brings relief to the secret wounds of our being. When we can express to God all that burdens our life and keeps us trapped beneath the weight of a judgment, then light is shed on the shadows within us. Knowing that we are listened to, understood, and forgiven by God is one of the sources of peace...and our hearts begin to find healing.

June 8

Neither misfortunes nor the injustice of poverty come from God; all God can do is give his love. And so we are filled with astonishment when we discover that God looks at every human being with infinite tenderness and deep compassion.

June 9

Jesus, our hope, your compassion is without limit. We are thirsting for your presence, as you tell us: "Why be afraid? Have no fear; I am here."[5]

June 10

Saying yes to God for life is fire. Six centuries before the coming of Christ, the prophet Jeremiah already realized this. In discouragement he said, "I will no longer think about God; I will no longer speak in his name...." But the day came when he could write, "There was a consuming fire within me, in the deepest part of my being. I wanted to repress it but could not."[6]

June 11

Across the earth, women, men, and young people are ferments of reconciliation right in the midst of the divisions that are tearing apart the human family. Filled with trust, they have everything to restore courage to those who were sunk in doubt and disenchantment, to support a fine human hope. Will we be among them?

June 12

God of mercy, you allow us to glimpse you through the life of your Christ.[7] *Through him, you give us this clear certainty: your love is above all compassion.*

June 13

When we pray and nothing seems to happen, does our prayer remain unanswered? No. In quiet trust in God, all prayer finds some kind of fulfillment. Perhaps it is different than we expected.... Does not God answer us with a view to a greater love?[8]

June 14

Children can be wounded by tensions in their family, by explanations given by adults in their presence. They can feel rejected, and this engenders an inner appeal not to be abandoned. The question often comes to mind: What has happened in this child? Could he or she have been humiliated at school, on the street, or somewhere else?

Will someone be there to help them find their way through a void that is affecting them in their heart of hearts? Listening to a child or an adolescent requires discretion and tact so as not to make their wounds any bigger.

June 15

Although there may well be shocks and even upheavals in our lives, Jesus the Christ is present by his Holy Spirit. He will always say to us: "Even when you are going through the harshest trial, I am present underneath your despair…and I am also there deep within your hope."

June 16

Holy Spirit, in every situation we would like to welcome you with great simplicity. And it is above all through the heart that you enable us to penetrate the mystery of your invisible presence at the center of our soul.

June 17

When Jesus, risen from the dead, says in his Gospel "I give you my peace,"[9] he is not offering us a life with no inner struggles. He invites us to realize that our hearts find peace especially by being rooted in the spirit of mercy.

June 18

While you are lingering far from God and even go to the point of forgetting him, he is already searching for you. And on his lips are these stupefying words: "In you I have placed my joy."[10]

June 19

Holy Spirit, mystery of a presence, your voice makes itself heard at the heart of our hopes as well as our sorrows. You tell us: "Be opened!"[11] *And even if we are almost without words, we can find that a single word is enough to pray.*

June 20

In the art of music, it sometimes happens that what cannot be expressed in words draws us to contemplation. A work by Bach, for example, can allow us to perceive all human longing. And the veil is lifted on the hidden God of Scripture.

June 21

Saint John writes these surprising words: "Among you stands someone whom you do not know."[12] Who is this "someone"? It is Christ, the Risen Lord. We may hardly be aware of him, yet he remains close beside every human being.

June 22

Happy those who root their lives in the trusting of faith! They will discover the most far-reaching mystery of all: the continual presence of God.

June 23

God, our Father, we want to love you with all our strength, with all our soul.[13] *But you know that there can be resistances within us. Give us the boldness to leap over these walls, to dare to renew again and again the yes of the gift of our life.*

June 24

John the Baptist already had this intuition: the coming of Christ is not just for a few people but for all. That is one of the joyful messages of the Gospel.[14]

June 25

What God gives sometimes seems so great...and we feel so poor! He offers us what we can scarcely imagine: Christ, and the Holy Spirit, come to dwell within our hearts, irresistibly.

June 26

There are parts of the world where the faith is in decline. Where there is a void, currents of religiosity of the most variegated sort can develop. As a consequence, one question remains constantly on our mind: How can we prepare the continuities of Christ where signs of his presence are disappearing?

June 27

Bless us, Christ Jesus. You come to comfort our hearts when the incomprehensible happens—the suffering of the innocent.

June 28

In the second century, Irenaeus, a Christian of the third generation, had the clear certainty of a communion in Christ. He left us these lines: "The splendor of God is a human being fully alive. The life of a human being is the contemplation of God."[15]

June 29

How aware are we of this? There is happiness in the humble gift of oneself. And something beyond all our hopes arises. The day comes when we are granted what we never even expected. The roads in shadow, the long nights with almost no light, lie behind us. Situations of struggle, and even dead ends, far from weakening us, can even help us to be built up within.

June 30

"Love your enemies, do good to those who hate you, pray for those who speak ill of you."[16] To understand these words of Christ, we must have made our way through inner deserts….

July

July 1

Risen Jesus, give us a steadfast heart that remains faithful to you. And if we wonder, "Is this possible?," your Gospel opens our eyes to your love: it is forgiveness, it is inner light.

July 2

To go forward in trust in God, it is a good idea to cling to a few Gospel realities and to return to them constantly: "In all things, peace of heart, joy, simplicity, mercy."

July 3

What if doubt were to take us by surprise? That shouldn't bring us to a standstill! Even when Jesus was on earth, right beside him there were disciples experiencing doubt. To one of them he said, "Happy those who believe without having seen!"[1]

July 4

To communicate Christ, is there any light more transparent than a life steeped in forgiveness and in infinite goodness, in which reconciliation is lived out day after day?

July 5

God of all loving, we are longing to hear your call resound in us: "Arise, let your soul live!" We never wish to choose darkness or discouragement, but to welcome the radiance of praise.

July 6

If spiritual values in many countries were not being called into question, our community would not have been led to welcome, week after week, young people not just from the North, East, and South of Europe, but also from other continents.

Seeing all these young faces on our hill of Taizé, we realize that they come with vital questions: "What does Christ want from me? How can I find a meaning for my life in him?" Without always sensing it clearly, they are trying to follow Christ.

The important thing for my brothers and myself is to respond to their trust by being, above all, men of prayer and of listening, never spiritual masters.

July 7

At the same period as Pope John XXIII, in Constantinople there was a man of the same prophetic vein, the Orthodox Patriarch Athenagoras. During a visit to him, what raised our hopes was the awareness that that 86-year-old man—with so few means at his disposal and enmeshed in a complex political situation—could have an enormous impact both close at hand and far away. He had the greatness of the truly generous. He had not been spared trials. In spite of everything, he remained hopeful. "When I enter my bedroom in the evening," he told us, "I leave my worries at the door and I say: We'll see tomorrow!"

July 8

A believer of the first centuries wrote, "Don't be anxious!"[2] When we entrust to Christ the worries that keep us far from him, he enables us to discover this reality: "In calm and trust will be your strength."[3]

July 9

Jesus, Love of all loving, you were always in me and I was forgetting you. You were in my heart of hearts, and I was looking for you elsewhere. When I kept myself far from you, you were waiting for me. And now I dare to tell you: "Christ, you are my life."

July 10

In human beings there is often a fathomless thirst for freedom. Like the most beautiful of coins, it can have another side. What kind of freedom would it be if, used in a self-centered way, it harmed the freedom of others? Freedom is intimately linked to forgiveness and reconciliation.

July 11

How much spiritual tact, how much attention, is necessary so that a fear of God does not enter a child's heart! "God is love."[4] If a life rooted in God meant fear of punishment, where would the Gospel be?

July 12

At every age, there is a need for periods of ripening. They take time. Why be impatient with oneself? Going from one beginning to another, from one stage to another, can open a way forward beyond discouragements.

July 13

Risen Christ, when we have the simple desire to welcome your love, little by little a flame is kindled in the depths of our being. Fueled by the Holy Spirit, it may be quite faint at first, but it keeps on burning. And when we realize that you love us, the trust of faith becomes our own song.

July 14

Letting the Risen Christ dwell within us and living intensely in the present moment.... His words are so clear: "Today, I would like to enter your home."[5] Today, not tomorrow.

July 15

Every human being yearns to be loved as well as to love. It is not for nothing that the Gospel alerts us about not withdrawing in isolation.

July 16

When we pray, reflections and images often pass through our minds. When we are surprised to find ourselves saying, "My thoughts are wandering; my heart is distracted," the Gospel replies, "God is greater than your heart."[6]

July 17

Holy Spirit, your presence is offered to everyone, and in you we find the consolation with which you can flood our lives. And we sense that, in prayer, we can entrust everything to you.

July 18

Though they are not so easy to grasp at first sight, will we let these words of Christ question us: "Whoever gives their life for love of me will find it."?[7] How will we find it? In an existence full of attentiveness and kindness of heart. And Christ himself will become our life.

July 19

When the night becomes dense, His love is a fire. Then what was glowing underneath the ashes bursts into flame.

July 20

Nothing is more harrowing than the break-up of a deep human affection. Sometimes the heart no longer knows where it is. To protect itself, to suffer less, it may become hardened. When Christ was rejected, he did not rebel. And it is this Christ whom we are following.

July 21

Jesus, our peace, if our lips keep silent, our heart listens to you and also speaks to you. And you say to each one of us: surrender yourself in all simplicity to the Holy Spirit; for this, the little bit of faith you have is enough.

July 22

Dostoyevsky allows us to glimpse deep-seated doubts within him, but his love for Christ is not thereby called into question: "My 'hosanna' has passed through the crucible of doubt."[8] His doubt was like a purifying fire that opened the way for a reflection of Christ to penetrate deep within him.

July 23

God of all eternity, whether we know it or not, your Holy Spirit is light within us. It illuminates the dark shadows of our soul, suffusing them with an invisible presence.

July 24

A heart filled with compassion makes us able to pray even for those who disfigure our intentions.

July 25

The call to follow Christ places us before an alternative: the choice between all or nothing. There is no middle ground. Even when a fog of hesitations catches us unawares, we would like to listen to him when he tells us, "Come and follow me. I will lead you to the wellsprings of living water,[9] the wellsprings of the Gospel."

July 26

Jesus, our peace, you never abandon us. And the Holy Spirit always opens a way forward, the way that consists of casting ourselves into God, fathomless depths of compassion.

July 27

Will we be among those who, even all alone, keep on praying in a church? How often has one single person been enough so that others can take over one day?

July 28

Today, for the multitudes of Christians who are innocent of these divisions that have occurred in the course of history, is it not urgent to bring to life a Gospel joy, the joy of living as people who are reconciled each day anew?

July 29

God of mercy, you are familiar with our longing to be a reflection of your presence and to make life beautiful for those you entrust to us.

July 30

There are those who end their lives in great isolation. Some even think they have achieved nothing. Who will pray for them, asking the Holy Spirit to console them?

July 31

Consenting over and over again to the trials that are so often part of human life. Searching for peace of heart in all things. And life becomes beautiful...yes, life will be beautiful. And then something we never dared hope for appears.

August

August 1

Christ Jesus, we are searching for your face. The look in your eyes is enough to dispel sorrow and worry. And by your Holy Spirit, you communicate to us new intuitions, sometimes quite unpretentious ones.

August 2

When we wake up each morning, if the spirit of praise were to fill our hearts, then in the monotony of daily life, an inner surge of vitality could arise.

August 3

In this period of history, there is an unprecedented awakening of the Christian conscience with regard to suffering throughout the world. Close to the forgotten of this earth, more and more people are looking for solutions and responses. Faith leads them to take on responsibilities for others.

August 4

Jesus, our joy, you want us to have hearts that are simple, a kind of springtime of the heart. And then the complications of existence do not paralyze us so much. You tell us: "Don't worry; I am with you always."

August 5

Why should someone who is ill or elderly worry and say, "I am not doing anything for others."? Could they have forgotten that their humble prayer is welcomed in God?

August 6

A Gospel revolution in our lives: Christ enters into us by the Holy Spirit, even passing through the contradictory forces over which our will has little control. He places a reflection of his face within us, transfiguring what troubles us about ourselves. In all things, peace of heart.

August 7

Holy Spirit, you breathe upon what is fragile. You kindle a flame of living charity that, within us, is still alive under the ashes. And through you, even the fears and the nights of our heart can become the dawn of a new life.

August 8

To discover a hope, don't we need most of all "living icons," witnesses to the trusting of faith?

August 9

In the Gospel, one day Jesus said to his disciples, "Let little children come to me; the Kingdom of God is for those who are like them."[1] Is not Christ utterly accessible to a simple heart?

August 10

In the course of a dialogue, when we are contradicted, even brusquely, we can find peace of heart by entrusting to the Holy Spirit those we are speaking with—and doing this, naturally, without their even realizing it.

August 11

Jesus of mercy, you invite us to be in communion with you. And our hearts rejoice when we realize that no one is excluded either from your forgiveness or your love.

August 12

Some areas of the world are desert regions for faith. But at the same time, there are believers who move mountains of indifference around them when they are invigorated by the freshness of life according to the Gospel.

August 13

In contemplative life, when the essential seems hidden from our eyes, that only makes us all the more desirous to discover the one reality: the mysterious presence of God in us.

August 14

God of peace, your Gospel makes us sensitive to those who experience violence, persecution, exile. And you call us to alleviate the sufferings in the human family.

August 15

It is not necessarily the powerful of the earth who determine the changes in the world. Could the Virgin Mary have thought that her yes to God would be so essential? Like her, so many of the humble of the earth are preparing ways of peaceful trust.

August 16

Even while providing for material needs, a parent can be absent for all practical purposes. Alluding to the parable of the prodigal son, a young New Yorker stated, "In my family it wasn't the son who went away; it was the father who left us."

August 17

Rooting our lives in the Holy Spirit means rediscovering at every age the Gospel in its first freshness.... Then there is no day that cannot be God's today.

August 18

Holy Spirit, in your presence we are never alone. Still more, a thirst fills our soul—to surrender everything to you.

August 19

A spirit of festival drawn from the Gospel is not euphoria. Enthusiasm, yes, but not something forced.... In all things, serene joy.

August 20

One day almost nine centuries before Christ, in the middle of a famine, a woman from the village of Zarephath saw Elijah, the man of God, come into her house. All the food that remained was a little flour and oil. To make him welcome, the widow did not hesitate to make three cakes with what she had left. And the unexpected happened... the flour and the oil would not run out.[2]

Isn't this a parable for our lives? With almost nothing, with very little, we can live something beyond all our hopes, something that will never come to an end.

August 21

Christ Jesus, you ask us the question: "Do you recognize the path of life open for you?" We want to remain filled with such beautiful trust in you, Christ, that we can discover the way you look at our lives with compassion.

August 22

When wounds from a recent or distant past become a burden, being listened to can be the beginning of a healing of the soul. And the breath of a trust arises.

August 23

For the person most devoid of knowledge, just as for the most cultivated, faith remains a humble trusting in God. If faith were to become a spiritual pretension, it would lead nowhere.

August 24

Your aspiration is to follow Christ. By what sign can you recognize that you have encountered him? When, as you search for him in prayer, your inner struggles do not harden you but lead you to the very wellsprings of his love. And a way forward takes shape: it always leads from worries towards trusting in God.

August 25

O Christ, you open our eyes to the wonder of your compassion. And we welcome your call as you say to us: "Come, follow me, in me you will find rest."

August 26

God is Spirit, and his presence remains invisible. He lives within us always, in times of darkness as well as when everything is bathed in light.

August 27

In contemplative prayer, it is up to us to keep on waiting "until day breaks and the morning star rises in our hearts."[3] And an imperceptible inner transformation, a transfiguration of our being, continues our whole life long.

August 28

Christ dwells in us! Do we not need time to prepare ourselves inwardly to grasp this Gospel reality, almost inaccessible to human thought?

August 29

Holy Spirit, you make it possible for us to cross the deserts of the heart. By your forgiveness, "you dissipate our faults like the morning mist."[4] There we find Christian freedom; there lies the wonder of a love.

August 30

How could my brothers and I live in the West if some of us were not present in the midst of the poorest in the Southern continents? Remembering that some of our brothers are sharing in living conditions of great poverty stimulates in us a call to simplicity: being simple in our daily lives, in the trust that we bring to one another.

August 31

For whoever knows how to love and say it with their life, existence is filled with serene beauty. Some days may bring disappointments, bitter tastes—accidents that can cause peace of heart to vanish. But every day there remains the possibility to surrender ourselves in God. A day is full when the worst that comes does not manage to halt the momentum towards fulfillment.

September

September 1

Nothing is more enduring than the memory of past humiliations and wounds. Such memories foster an attitude of suspiciousness, sometimes lasting several generations. Gospel forgiveness, on the other hand, enables us to go beyond the memory. Will we be among those who gather up their energies to curb all forms of mistrust, be they age-old or brand-new?

September 2

God of mercy, enable us to surrender ourselves to you in silence and in love. Such trust does not come easily to our human condition. But you open within us the way that leads towards the radiance of a hope.

September 3

Would our life be subject to the whims of fate or to a blind destiny? Far from it! Our life finds meaning when it is, above all, the living response to a call from God.

September 4

The Holy Spirit has the strength to sustain a yes for our whole life. Has he not placed in us a desire for eternity and the infinite? In the Spirit, at every age, it is possible to find new vitality and to say to ourselves, "Be steadfast of heart and keep going forward!"[1]

September 5

Many Western Christians love their Eastern brothers and sisters, on the one hand because of all the trials they have gone through, and also because in them there are such transparent gifts of communion. A Russian Orthodox bishop, the late Metropolitan Nikodim of Saint Petersburg, still remains one of these witnesses for us. He came to Taizé already in 1962. He bore in his heart the hope of a communion. By his life, he helped us understand that the secret of the Orthodox soul is found, above all, in a prayer open to contemplation.

Goodness of heart is a vital reality for so many Orthodox Christians. By their trust in the Holy Spirit, by their focus on the resurrection, they strengthen us in the essential of the faith. We try to be very attentive to the young people from Russia, Belarus, Ukraine, Greece, Romania, Serbia, and Bulgaria who come to Taizé.

September 6

Jesus, joy of our hearts, when the desire to fulfill what you expect of us comes welling up inside us, we realize that you invite us to love, just as you love us.[2]

September 7

Attempting to live for Christ in the midst of others, we pray to be able to forgive and forgive again. There is found the extreme of loving.

September 8

One day when my Indian goddaughter, Marie-Sonaly, was five years old, she and I found a small icon of the Virgin and child. That image spoke to us beyond measure. It was the symbol of a mother's welcome. We were able to understand that her mother, like every mother who has already entered the life of eternity, continues to welcome us along with Mary, the mother of Jesus.

September 9

Prayer opens us up to a boundless communion. With no beginning nor end, the realities of God, of Christ, of the Holy Spirit, cannot be measured. The Holy Spirit fills the universe.

September 10

Holy Spirit, inner light, you shine in the happy days as well as in the times in our life when we undergo trials. And when the daylight seems to disappear, your presence remains.

September 11

When someone very close to us dies, the trial can go so far as to undermine our hope. Rediscovering the trusting of faith and peace of heart sometimes requires having a great deal of patience with ourselves. When we need to be comforted, Christ sends the Holy Spirit, the Comforter. And the pain of a separation can be transfigured into a communion that is at one and the same time so mysterious and so indispensable.

September 12

Doesn't a contemplative outlook, focused on God, rescue us from the greyness of routine, from monotony? Permeated by the Gospel, such an outlook is also capable of perceiving the treasures of a heart warmed by infinite goodness.

September 13

There were periods in history when some Christians were particularly sensitive to sharing. In the fourth century, Saint John Chrysostom wrote, "Quarrels and wars break out because some people try to take for themselves what belongs to everyone. It is as if nature became indignant that human beings, by means of those cold words 'yours' and 'mine,' have sowed division where God has set unity."

September 14

God of mercy, when it is hard for us to trust in you, why should we worry? Being in your presence in a peaceful silence is already praying. And you understand all that we are. Even a sigh can be a prayer.

September 15

When faith is not awakened at an early age, a space remains empty inside us. Who will find ways to open up children and young people to trust in Christ? Kneel down with a child before an icon, praying in silence…and he or she can be awakened to the mystery of God. An intuition of faith, no matter how feeble, even if it has been forgotten, often reappears later on in life.

September 16

As we remember Christ's call again and again, will we make our life a response to it, a response of wonder?

September 17

When the weight of a discouragement overwhelms you to the point of abandoning Christ, will you put off coming back to the inner oasis in your heart of hearts, that intimate place where God is everything?

September 18

Christ of compassion, we dare to tell you everything. Enable us to speak to you at times like the child we used to be.

September 19

One day, Christ blessed five loaves of bread and distributed them to everyone without distinction.[3] Long ago, this story inspired Christians to discover a sign of hospitality: giving blessed bread to all those, believers or non-believers, who for different reasons do not receive the Eucharist. The Orthodox churches were the first to open this road.

September 20

When that communion which is the Church becomes transparent by striving to love and to forgive, it enables Gospel realities to shine through with the freshness of springtime. Will we enter soon into a springtime of the Church?

September 21

There are vast numbers of people who come close to the holiness of Christ by the gift of their lives. They have heard the words Jesus speaks to each person: "Come, follow me!"[4]

September 22

God of all eternity, open in us the gates of your mercy. And then we realize that the will of your love is not a law written on tablets of stone. It is rather burning charity, written in our hearts.[5]

September 23

We are often asked why so many young people come to Taizé? What answer can we give? It was unexpected. The years pass, and we are no less astonished. Gradually we realized that it was essential to live in a mutual trust with the younger generations. We wanted with all our hearts to see a capacity for trust come to fruition in the young; it is a lever to provide a way out of a crisis of confidence in humanity.

Sometimes we ask ourselves whether the welcome we offer here is not too rudimentary, too poor. And we discover that with great simplicity of heart and with very few resources, we are enabled to accomplish a Gospel hospitality that did not seem possible.

September 24

Others can recognize our trust in God when we express it by the simple giving of our own lives. Faith becomes credible and is passed on, above all, when it is lived out.

September 25

Could there be chasms of the unknown in us, and also an abyss of guilt that comes from who knows where? God never threatens anyone, and the forgiveness with which he floods our lives comes to bring healing to our soul.

September 26

Christ Jesus, your call is to a vocation for an entire lifetime. And so, even if we are unfamiliar with your Gospel, *we sense that you are inviting us to welcome you forever.*

September 27

The Gospel awakens us to compassion and to kind-heartedness without bounds. There is nothing naive about this; it can require vigilance. And these values lead to a discovery: seeking to make others happy liberates us from ourselves.

September 28

A Christian who lived sixteen hundred years ago, Saint Augustine, left behind some words that open wide the gates of the Gospel. He struggled a great deal to come to God. He suffered from his behavior as a young man. He was so honest with himself that at times he must have despaired of his own self. Then one day, he was able to write down these words: "If you desire to know God, you already have faith."[6]

September 29

In whoever lives the first of the Beatitudes, "Happy the simple in heart,"[7] Christ allows the light of the Gospel to shine, incomparably. And simplicity brings to birth, spontaneously, a peaceful joy.

September 30

Christ Jesus, in the Gospel you ask the question: "Who am I for you?"[8] You are the one who keeps on searching for us. In your life on earth, you were affected to the depths of your being; you wept at the death of someone you loved.[9] And for you, Christ, loving culminates in kindheartedness.

October

October 1

Is not humble prayer within the reach of everyone? The apostle Paul was aware of this when he wrote, "We do not know how to pray, but the Holy Spirit comes to help us in our inability and prays within us."[1]

October 2

An equal trust shown to all the peoples of the earth, and not just to some, opens a way to peace. In every nation, there is a small number of demented persons who are capable, if they come to power, of drawing the masses into the vortex of hatred and war. For this reason, it is crucial never to humiliate members of a nation when a few of its leaders have triggered unbelievable violence. Are we sufficiently aware that no one people is guiltier than others—such a thing does not exist, and never shall.

October 3

Jesus, peace of our hearts, where the trusting of faith has been shaken, make us bearers of your Gospel and keep us close to those who are beset by doubts.

October 4

There are countless Christians who would like to be bearers of peace in that communion of love that is the Church. They are not naive when confronted with abuses that undermine communion, but they strive for silence and love with all their soul.

October 5

Trust in Christ is not conveyed by means of arguments that attempt to persuade at all costs and, thus, end up causing anxiety.

October 6

The Holy Spirit never leaves our soul; even at death, communion with God remains. Knowing that God welcomes us into his love forever becomes a source of peaceful trust.

October 7

God of mercy, we are longing for the breath of your Holy Spirit. He causes a spring of living water to well up, a Gospel *joy, even in the contradictions of our heart.*

October 8

In the Gospel, Christ enters into solidarity with the incomprehensible suffering of the innocent. Did he not come to earth so every human being might know that he or she is loved?

October 9

In the Gospel, Christ never calls us to sadness or gloom. On the contrary, he places peaceful joy within our reach, and even jubilation in the Holy Spirit.

October 10

Christ Jesus, at the wellsprings of trust in you, you enable us to find peace of heart, which is so essential in order to receive life from you and to build ourselves up within.

October 11

In the most somber moments, when there is intense discouragement among Christians, what else can we do except abandon ourselves to the hope that springs from faith?

October 12

Before the universe began, from all eternity, Christ was in God. Since the birth of humanity, he has been a living Word.[2] Then he dwelt among us on earth as a poor man. Risen from the dead, by the Holy Spirit he remains alongside each person.

October 13

We do not forgive in order to change the other person. That would be a stratagem that has nothing to do with the selfless love found in the Gospel. We forgive on account of Christ. Forgiving means not even seeking to know what the other person will do with that forgiveness.

October 14

Jesus, our joy, because your forgiveness radiates trust, peace of heart is possible and even certain. Your Gospel tells us: "Why be upset? You can change nothing by worrying about it, add neither a cubit to your height nor a day to your life."[3]

October 15

The essence of prayer never changes, yet it can take on a host of different expressions. There are people who pray in a great silence. Others need many words. Saint Theresa of Avila wrote, "When I speak to the Lord, often I do not know what I am saying." Others find heaven's joy on earth, a fulfillment, in prayer together with other people.

October 16

Are we going to listen to the call that comes to us right from the time of the Gospel: "Do not put out the Spirit's flame."?[4] Penetrated as we are by the breath of the Holy Spirit, will we realize that the Spirit is at work within us, bringing us out of darkness and leading us towards the light?

October 17

To those who seek you, Christ Jesus, you give peace of heart. This peace is there, close at hand, in the compassion with which you regard each of our lives.

October 18

Luke's Gospel ends with the account of the disciples bowing low with their foreheads to the ground.[5] In this way, they take up a prayer posture that perhaps goes back to the remotest origins of humanity. It expresses the silent offering of one's life.

October 19

Does it not sometimes happen that, without realizing it, the older generations prepare a way forward for the young towards trust in God? Young people from Estonia said: "If we have become believers and if we are here in Taizé, it is because of our grandmothers. Most of them were sent away from their country for many years. Over there, in the place to which they were deported, all they had to keep them going was faith. They are simple women. They did not understand the reason for so much suffering. Some have come back; they are transparent and without bitterness. For us now, they are saints."

October 20

For a life to be beautiful, extraordinary abilities or great expertise are not required. There is happiness in the humble giving of oneself.

October 21

God of mercy, you never stop searching for all who have distanced themselves from you. And by your forgiveness, you call us to sing: a thirst fills my soul, a thirst to surrender everything in you.

October 22

Could you have forgotten the presence of God in you? Rest in him, express an intention...and you will find him wherever you happen to be, at home, at work, in a street filled with the noise of traffic....

October 23

Where is the source of hope and of joy? It is in God, who tirelessly seeks us out and finds in us the profound beauty of the human soul.

October 24

Through the face of a human being, especially when tears and sufferings have made it more transparent, it becomes possible to glimpse a reflection of the face of Christ himself.

October 25

Breath of God's loving, Holy Spirit, if we place our trust in you, it is because you lead us to discover this surprising reality: God creates neither fear nor anguish in us; all God can do is love.

October 26

Prayer is a serene force; it keeps us from growing unfeeling in the face of the turmoil experienced by whole sectors of the human family. From it are drawn vital energies of compassion.

October 27

In the course of our Christian life, we are enabled to pass from one beginning to another beginning. But this process burns out if it does not draw its energy from an underlying continuity—the invisible presence of the Holy Spirit in us.

October 28

While prayer alone can be arduous, the beauty of prayer with others is an incomparable support to the inner life. By means of simple words, hymns, songs, it communicates a discreet and silent joy.

October 29

Risen Jesus, in the ploughed-up earth of our lives, you come to place the trusting of faith. A small seed at first, it can become within us one of the most unmistakable Gospel realities. It sustains the inexhaustible goodness of a human heart.

October 30

God understands our words and our silences, too. So often silence is all there is to prayer.

October 31

The vast possibilities of science and technology are able to alleviate sufferings, and to mitigate famines. Indispensable though they may be, however, these powerful means by themselves are not enough. If we were to wake up one fine morning in societies that were functional, highly technological, but where the confidence of faith, the intelligence of the heart, and a thirst for reconciliation had been extinguished, what then would be the future of the human family?

November

November 1

Living God, we praise you for the multitudes of women, men, young people, and children who, across the earth, are striving to be witnesses to peace, trust, and reconciliation. In the steps of the holy witnesses of all the ages, from the apostles and the Virgin Mary down to those of today, enable us day after day to dispose ourselves inwardly to place our trust in the Mystery of the Faith.

November 2

Trust in the resurrection enables us to realize that a communion between believers is not interrupted by death. In simplicity of heart, we can ask those we love and who have gone before us into eternity's life, "Pray for me; pray with me." During their life on earth, their prayer supported us. After their death, how could we stop relying on them?

November 3

One of the fruits of the Holy Spirit in us is joy.[1] When there is a deep-seated joy, the Holy Spirit is present.

November 4

Holy Spirit, Spirit of consolation, our heart of hearts is longing to be permeated by a peaceful faith. Illuminated by your light, we glimpse the mystery of our life, and the nights of the soul are dispelled.

November 5

Baptized in the Holy Spirit, we have been clothed in Christ forever. And God can say to each one of us, "You are the only one for me; in you, I find my joy."[2] In the tenth century, a Christian named Simeon wrote, "Christ will come to each person as if he were concerned with that person alone."

November 6

When some people experience an inner void, they wonder, "But where is God?"[3] And yet does not Christ remain alongside each person, even those who are unaware of him?

November 7

Jesus, our hope, enable us to hear your voice saying: "I, Christ, love you." That is the source of peace of heart.

November 8

Everywhere across the earth, Christians are intent on assuming responsibilities, often very specific ones, to make the earth a better place to live in. And how astonishing it is to discover all that is made possible by a love drawn from the wellsprings of trust in God!

November 9

Could you be going through one of those periods when everything seems to be all dried up? At such times when nothing seems to be happening in you, with very little, a desert flower can blossom.

November 10

Savior of every life, let those who are seeking you rejoice. In one of the pages of the Gospel you tell us: "I am familiar with your trials and your poverty, and yet you are filled."[4] *Filled by what? By the living springs hidden in the depths of each person.*

November 11

Christ knows what an inner combat we can sometimes wage in order to be found transparent. This struggle within is a sign of our love for him. But our life is not one of constant struggle. As we welcome the Gospel's message of joy, the Holy Spirit brings us what we often did not expect—peace of heart, and with it a happiness.

November 12

Praised be the Holy Spirit for loving us always, even when we feel nothing—or almost nothing—of his continual presence.

November 13

Risen Jesus, mystery of a presence, you never want us to be tormented; you clothe us in your peace. And a Gospel joy comes to touch the depths of the soul.

November 14

Among the children who often come to the prayer services in Taizé, one day there was a brother and a sister. The little girl, totally absorbed, kept her hands folded; her lips whispered a few words. The little boy, his hands over his eyes, remained silent. With or without words, their faces and gestures expressed the beauty of an inner life.

November 15

In the great troubles of our life, the Holy Spirit is a support, a comfort, in whom the wellsprings of jubilation, of joy light as a feather, are always offered. And this joy brings us closer to those who are going through suffering.

November 16

There is no technique for praying; there is no method to achieve inner silence. If our prayer is only stammering, that hardly matters. Are we not, all of us, poor people of the Gospel?

November 17

Living God, however poor our prayer is, we search for you with confidence. And your compassion carves out a way forward through our hesitations and even through our doubts.

November 18

The Gospel speaks of a young man who was seeking the will of God's love. He came to Christ with his questions. Jesus replied to him, "You are lacking one thing: sell what you have, give it to the poor, then come, follow me." And the young man went away sad.[5] Why? He did not have the inner freedom to give himself.

November 19

"Christ Jesus, light of my heart, do not let my darkness speak to me."[6] In writing that prayer, Saint Augustine had this intuition: When our inner darkness attracts all our attention, we begin to converse incessantly—not with the Risen Christ, but with what hurts us in ourselves. Where can that lead? Nowhere at all.

November 20

God of mercy, when we understand that nothing can separate us from you, trust in you opens for us the road that leads upward towards a peace-filled joy.

November 21

Icons can enhance the beauty of prayer. They are like windows open on the realities of God. There are artists' hands that give us a glimpse of Gospel reflections; they know how to make the mystery of God accessible to our eyes.

November 22

The apostle Peter saw Jesus during his life on earth. But with the deep realism of his faith, he knew well that "we love Christ without having seen him and, though we still do not see him, we place our trust in him." And he could go on to write, "You are filled with a joy beyond words that already transfigures you."[7]

November 23

Will we be among those who spread the fine hope of a new future? To prepare this, who will open up ways of conciliation where hatred and violence are exploding?

November 24

Christ of all compassion, you enable us to turn to you...and an inner light rises in our hearts.[8] *Then, to pray, these few words are enough: Jesus, my joy, my hope, and my life.*

November 25

Happy those who draw from God a trust that will never die away, that will never wear out!

November 26

Forgiving is one of the most unbelievable, one of the most indispensable Gospel realities for anyone who wants to follow Christ. And a heart overflowing with kindness is sometimes close to a miracle in our lives.

November 27

Holy Spirit, the Gospel assures us that your presence is within us.[9] *It is as sure as our own existence.*

November 28

One day, Jesus spoke grave words regarding "those who lay heavy burdens on other people's shoulders but are unwilling to lift a finger themselves to move them."[10]

November 29

To respond to Christ's call to the very end, prepare yourself for long periods of faithfulness. In you will be forged, not an illusory love that would be satisfied with words, but a soul permeated with kindness.

November 30

Some parents are concerned when they see their children leaving the places where they themselves pray. But will not the best of their faith appear again when the children grow up and have to take on important responsibilities? The fine flower of trust in God, glimpsed in childhood, is not lost forever. Its scent pervades the soul, invisibly.

December

December 1

Whoever responds to the Gospel's calls refuses to consider anyone an enemy.[1] Praying in silence and love, they find enough freedom even to forgive those who are distorting their intentions.

December 2

Holy Spirit, mystery of a presence, you penetrate the depths of our being, and there you discern a longing. You know what our intention is—to communicate your compassion through an infinite goodness of heart.

December 3

However little we understand of the Gospel, it is light in our midst. However little we perceive of the Holy Spirit, he is life for us. However little we grasp of the Eucharist, it is Christ's presence in us.

December 4

Our heart finds peace in knowing that death is not the end. Death opens the way towards a life where God welcomes us to himself forever.

When she was already very elderly, my mother had a heart attack. As soon as she could speak again, she uttered these words: "I am not afraid of dying; I know who I believe in…but I love life." And on the day she died she whispered, "Life is beautiful…."

December 5

In prayer, God does not ask us to accomplish wonders that are beyond us. But God does enable us to surrender ourselves to him in great simplicity. And the Holy Spirit suggests simple words: "God of mercy, what do you want from me?"

December 6

There are people who, by giving themselves, attest that human beings are not doomed to hopelessness. Are we among them? However powerless we may be, are we not called to communicate a mystery of hope to those around us by the lives we lead?

December 7

God of all loving, you call us to live lives rooted in you. Even were we to leave you, by your Holy Spirit you remain in us. And your presence in us is not for one moment only, but for all time.

December 8

Through the Virgin Mary, the mystery of offering is revealed. A Puerto Rican woman understood this when she wrote the following words to her son as he was committing himself by a yes for his entire lifetime: "When I discovered your total love for God, I thought of the Virgin Mary. As a mother, she consented to what God had prepared. My son, what can I do when God is acting? I cannot refuse to give God what belongs to Him. You are all that I have but, because of the love God has for us, we give him everything."

December 9

The astonishing presence of the Holy Spirit is a fire. Even when it is a pale glimmer, suddenly it flares up within. It keeps on burning even when we have the impression that we do not know how to pray.

December 10

At times when the trusting of faith becomes hard to grasp, we can say to God, "Do not look at what little faith I have, but enable me to rely on the faith of your whole Church, on the faith of so many humble witnesses who have rooted their lives in you to a point beyond compare."

December 11

Christ, for each of us you desire joy, a happiness straight from the Gospel. And the peace of our heart can make life beautiful for those around us.

December 12

The Holy Spirit is always present, permeating our depths, enabling us to wait for God's joy to touch the deepest part of our soul.

December 13

The Holy Spirit, poured out on every human being, gives freedom and spontaneity. The Spirit restores a zest for life to those who had lost it, and comes to deliver us from discouragement. Neither doubts nor the impression that God is silent can take his Holy Spirit away from us.

December 14

The more we share with simplicity what we have, the more our hearts become welcoming for those around us. Simplifying more and more enables us to offer a welcome to others, even with very little.

December 15

Christ Jesus, enable us to heed your call to live each day as God's today.

December 16

Four centuries after Christ, Saint Augustine wrote these words, which remain more relevant than ever: "There is a voice of the heart and a language of the heart. This inner voice is our prayer when our lips are closed and our soul is open before God. We remain silent and our heart speaks—not to human ears, but to God. You can be sure that God will hear you."[2]

December 17

When we are called to speak about the Gospel or to pray aloud in front of others, if we could say to ourselves, "May your prayer and your words never contain a threat in the name of God!" God is love. He does not make use of fear to impose himself upon human beings. Even when Christ was mistreated, he did not threaten anyone.[3]

December 18

Holy Spirit, Spirit of consolation, if there are times when we are overwhelmed by inner loneliness, enable us to understand that Christ is always present and that he can always calm our hearts.

December 19

Throughout our life, we are beset with situations hard to explain; they sometimes include oppositions, departures, breaks in communion. And then we ask ourselves: "Will we let our joy fade away?" No, joy can remain even in times of difficulty. Instead of burdening others with our sadness, the joy of our heart brings happiness to those around us.

December 20

Who is this Christ we are following? He is the one who enables us to live in communion with him. By his Holy

Spirit, he remains alongside us—today, tomorrow, and always. In him, the wellsprings of jubilation never run dry.[4]

December 21

Some people are troubled by the impression that God is silent, as if his presence were linked to what we feel. But communion with God remains even when any detectable resonance is absent.

December 22

Holy Spirit, when we lay down our burdens and our trials in you, already you place peace of heart in our soul.

December 23

In the depths of our being is found a call to inner freedom. And in this freedom, there is poetry. It can find joy in a trifle—the wind in the trees, the play of light in the sky, the intimacy of a simple meal, the presence of those we love, of children....

December 24

If each night in our lives could become a kind of Christmas night, a night illuminated from within....

December 25

Jesus, son of the Virgin Mary, at Christmas you offer us the joyful message of your Gospel. All who listen, all who welcome the gifts of the Holy Spirit, by day as well as in the vigils of the night, discover that even with very little faith, with almost nothing, the essential is offered.

December 26

Not knowing how to make himself understood, God came to earth himself, poor and humble. If Christ Jesus had not lived among us, God would remain far off, inaccessible. Jesus allows us to see God shining through his life.[5]

December 27

Were it possible to fathom a human heart, the surprising thing would be to discover there the silent longing for a presence. In John's Gospel, there appears a response to this longing: "Someone you do not know is among you."[6] Is he not always in our midst, this Christ with whom we may be almost unacquainted?

December 28

How aware are we that, for God, human beings are "sacred by the wounded innocence of their childhood"?

December 29

Jesus, our joy, you tell us in your Gospel: "Look at the birds of the sky and the lilies of the field. Are you not worth more than they? Why be anxious?"[7]

December 30

As we go from one beginning to another, if we could prepare ourselves to welcome every new day as if it were unique...and Christ says to each person, "I will never leave you alone."[8]

December 31

In you, peace of heart, serene joy. The Holy Spirit has buried your past in the heart of Christ. And he will take care of your future.

Holy Spirit, do not let our hearts be troubled; reassure us in our night, grant us your joy.

Passages from the Bible dealing with Trust and Peace of Heart

In the midst of his suffering, Job said: "I know that my Redeemer is alive, and that at the end he will rise up upon the earth. After I awake, he will set me beside him."

—Job 19:25–26

In God alone my soul finds rest;
from him comes salvation.
In God alone my soul finds rest;
my hope comes from him.
Trust in him at all times, my people;
pour out your heart before him.
God is our refuge!

—Psalm 62:1, 5, 8

The Lord is kind and just;
our God is merciful.
The Lord watches over the simple:
I was weak, and he saved me.
Return, my soul, to your rest.

—Psalm 116:5–7

Lord, my heart is not proud;
I do not set my sights too high.
I do not run after great things,
things beyond my comprehension.
No, I have kept my soul still and quiet
like a child in its mother's arms;
like a little child, so is my soul within me.

—Psalm 131

The Lord says: "Your salvation is in returning and rest; your strength lies in quiet and in confident trust."

—Isaiah 30:15

"I know the plans I have for you," says the Lord. "Plans for peace and not for misfortune, to give you a future and hope."

—Jeremiah 29:11

The Lord says: "I will give you a new heart; I will place within you a new spirit. I will take from your bodies the heart of stone and give you a heart of flesh. I will place my spirit within you."

—Ezekiel 36:26–27

Jesus said: "Come to me all you who are weary and overburdened, and I will give you rest."

—Matthew 11:28

As the storm was shaking their boat, Jesus said to his disciples: "Courage! It is I; don't be afraid!"

—Matthew 14:27

Jesus said to his disciples: "Which of you can add a single hour to his life by worrying about it? If you cannot even do such a simple thing, what point is there in worrying about all the rest?"

—Luke 12:25–26

Jesus said to his disciples: "I have told you these things while I am still with you. But the Advocate, the Holy Spirit whom the Father will send in my name, will teach you everything and will remind you of all I said to you. I leave you peace; my peace is the gift I give you.... Do not let your hearts be troubled or afraid."

—John 14:25–27

Jesus said to his disciples: "I have told you these things so that in me you may have peace."

—John 16:33

Saint Paul wrote: "God's Reign is justice, peace, and joy in the Holy Spirit."

—Romans 14:17

Saint Paul wrote: "May God the Father strengthen your inner self through his Spirit. May he make Christ dwell in your hearts through faith so that, rooted and grounded in love, you may receive the ability to grasp, together with all God's holy people, what is the width, the length, the height, and the depth...and to know the love of Christ, which is beyond all knowledge, so that you may be filled to overflowing with all the fullness of God."

—Ephesians 3:16–19

Saint Paul wrote: "With all humility, gentleness, and patience, accept one another in love, eager to remain one in the Spirit, linked together by the bond of peace."

—Ephesians 4:2–3

Saint Paul wrote: "Once you were darkness; now you are light in the Lord. Conduct yourselves as people who belong to the light."

—Ephesians 5:8

Saint Paul wrote: "If there is any encouragement in belonging to Christ, any comfort in love, any communion in the Spirit, any affection and compassion, then make my joy complete by striving for the same goal, sharing the same love, being one in heart and soul."

—Philippians 2:1–2

Saint Paul wrote: "Rejoice in the Lord always! I will say it again: rejoice! Let everyone see how serene you are. The Lord is near. Do not worry about anything, but in all things, by means of prayers and petitions offered with thanksgiving, make known your requests to God. And the peace of God, which is beyond all understanding, will keep your hearts and minds rooted in Christ Jesus."

—Philippians 4:4–7

Saint Paul wrote: "As people chosen by God, holy and dearly loved, clothe yourselves in feelings of compassion, kindness, humility, gentleness, and patience. Put up with one another and forgive each other if anyone has a cause for complaint against anyone else; just as the Lord forgave you, you do the same. And over everything else put on love: that is the bond that unites them all perfectly. Let Christ's peace reign in your hearts; in it you have been called to form one body. And be grateful."

—Colossians 3:12–15

Saint Paul wrote: "Avoid irreverent and empty discussions, which only lead further and further away from God."

—2 Timothy 2:16

Saint James wrote: "No one who is being tempted should say, 'This temptation comes from God.' God cannot be tempted to do evil, and he never tempts anyone."

—James 1:13

Saint Peter wrote: "You love Christ although you have not seen him, and although you still do not see him, you believe, and are filled to overflowing with a joy too deep for words and radiant with God's glory."

—1 Peter 1:8b

Saint Peter wrote: "When insulted, Christ did not insult in return. When he suffered, he did not threaten, but placed his trust in God."

—1 Peter 2:23

Saint Peter wrote: "Entrust all your worries to God, since he takes care of you."

—1 Peter 5:7

Saint John wrote: "My little children, we must not love just in words or with our lips, but truly, by our actions. This is how we shall know that we belong to the truth, and in God's presence our hearts will be at peace even if our hearts condemn us, because God is greater than our hearts, and he knows everything."

—1 John 3:18–20

Saint John wrote: "God is love, and whoever remains in love remains in God and God in him.... When we love we have no fear, since perfect love casts out fear, and anyone who is still afraid of punishment has not reached the perfection of love."

—1 John 4:16b, 18

Notes

January

1. Matthew 11:28–29
2. 1 John 4:8, 16
3. John 3:17
4. Matthew 25:40
5. John 1:5
6. Psalm 62:1–2
7. John 14:27
8. 1 Kings 19:9–13
9. Encyclical *Redemptor Hominis*, 1979
10. Matthew 3:11
11. 1 Thessalonians 5:19
12. Psalm 42:7
13. Matthew 16:25

February

1. Luke 2:22–24
2. John XXIII, *Journal of a Soul*
3. Luke 9:62
4. 1 Peter 1:8
5. *Treatise on the Gospel of Luke*, V, 58
6. Matthew 11:28–29
7. *Letter to Diognetus*, VI

March

1. John 1:1–3
2. Luke 9:24
3. 2 Corinthians 4:7
4. Mark 4:27
5. Proverbs 30:16
6. Psalm 84:6
7. Luke 10:21
8. Luke 1:38
9. 1 Peter 5:7
10. Revelation 3:20 and Mark 10:21

Holy Week and Pentecost

1. Matthew 26:40–41
2. 1 Peter 2:23
3. Matthew 11:28
4. 1 Peter 3:18–20; 4:6
5. John 14:16, 26; 16:7

April

1. Mark 9:24
2. Luke 24:13–35
3. 1 John 3:20
4. John 21:15–17
5. John 21:15–17
6. Matthew 8:8

May

1. Matthew 5:8
2. Luke 2:19, 51
3. *Homily on Naboth the Poor Man*, 53

4. Matthew 5:44
5. Isaiah 53:2–4,7
6. 1 Peter 1:8
7. Matthew 5:23–24
8. John 3:17
9. Matthew 28:20
10. *Advice to Novices* (Erfurter Reden, Reden der Unterweisung)
11. John 14:18–20
12. Matthew 11:28
13. Luke 10:38–42
14. Romans 8:26

June

1. John 6:56
2. *Discourse to the Pastors of Rome*, February 1959
3. Matthew 25:40
4. *Letter to Diognetus*
5. Mark 4:40; 6:50
6. Jeremiah 20:9
7. John 14:9
8. 1 John 5:14–15
9. John 14:27; 20:19–21
10. Luke 15:20–32
11. Mark 7:34
12. John 1:26
13. Luke 10:27
14. Luke 3:6,18
15. *Adversus Haereses*, IV, 20, 7
16. Luke 6:27–28

July

1. John 20:29
2. Philippians 4:6
3. Isaiah 30:15
4. 1 John 4:8, 16
5. Luke 19:5
6. 1 John 3:20
7. Luke 9:24
8. *Notebooks*
9. Isaiah 49:10

August

1. Matthew 19:14
2. 1 Kings 17:7–16
3. 2 Peter 1:19
4. Isaiah 44:22

September

1. Sirach 2:2
2. John 15:12
3. Matthew 14:13–21
4. Mark 10:21
5. Jeremiah 31:33; 2 Corinthians 3:3
6. *Commentary on Psalm 37*, 14
7. Matthew 5:3
8. Matthew 16:15
9. John 11:35

October

1. Romans 8:26
2. John 1:1–10
3. Matthew 6:27
4. 1 Thessalonians 5:19
5. Luke 24:52

November

1. Galatians 5:22
2. Mark 1:11
3. Psalm 42:3
4. Revelation 2:9
5. Mark 10:17–22
6. *Confessions* 12, 10, 10
7. 1 Peter 1:8
8. 2 Peter 1:19
9. 1 Corinthians 3:16
10. Matthew 23:4

December

1. Matthew 5:44
2. *Commentary on Psalm 125*, 8
3. 1 Peter 2:23
4. Philippians 4:4
5. John 14:9
6. John 1:26
7. Matthew 6:25–34
8. Matthew 28:20

About the Taizé Community

In 1940 a young Swiss man settled in the tiny village of Taizé, France situated amid the Burgundy vineyards between the ancient monastic foundations of Cluny and Citeaux. He offered shelter and hiding to political refugees, particularly Jews. At the same time he gathered around him a few men of different Christian denominations, the beginnings of the great ecumenical community-to-be.

This new edition of *Peace of Heart* by Brother Roger has been entirely rewritten. It distills the message Taizé has offered throughout more than fifty years spent in community. How can we rediscover a fine human hope, and still more, hope in God, when our steps become heavy and disenchantment gains the upper hand?

The book has been written for everyone to whom the mission of Taizé appeals and particularly the young people who visit in such numbers during the summer months. It is a book to be kept, treasured, and consulted at regular intervals.